Still Finding The Way

Poems for a Generation in Search of
Meaning

iAjay J

BookLeaf
Publishing

India | USA | UK

Dedication

To everyone who's still finding their way.

To the dreamers, the believers, and the ones who refuse
to give up even when the road feels endless.
May these words remind you that being lost is just
another way of being on the path.

Preface

There are moments in life when silence speaks louder than words — when every question we ask becomes a mirror, and every answer takes us deeper into ourselves. This book was born in one of those moments.

Still Finding the Way is not a collection of perfect thoughts — it is a collection of honest ones. Each poem carries a fragment of what it means to be human in this restless age — to feel lost, to love deeply, to fall apart, to rebuild, and to keep walking even when the path isn't clear. These verses were written for every soul that has ever stayed awake wondering, *"Am I enough?"*

For every dreamer chasing light through their own shadows. For everyone who's still learning that growing doesn't mean having it all figured out — it means having the courage to keep going. As I wrote these poems, I realized that "finding the way" is not about reaching somewhere — it's about becoming someone. And maybe that's the quiet truth life tries to teach us all along: that the journey itself is the destination.

If, in these pages, you find even one line that feels like it was written for you — then I hope you know, you are not alone. You're still finding the way. And so am I.

— iAjay J.

Acknowledgements

This book is not mine alone.
It carries the voices, faces, and stories of so many
who walked beside me — knowingly or not —
while I searched for meaning through words.

To my **students**, who remind me every day that
learning and growing never stop — your courage
and curiosity inspired many of these lines. You are
the heart of this journey.
To my **friends and mentors**, who believed in my
writing long before I did — your faith lit the lamp
when I was lost in my own doubts.
To my **family**, for their patience, love, and quiet
strength — you are my roots, even when the
winds of life tried to scatter me.
And finally, to every **reader** who picks up this book
with an open heart — thank you. You complete
the circle between writer and world.

May these poems be a soft place to rest, a spark of
light when the road feels dark, and a reminder
that it's okay to not have it all figured out.
After all — we are all *still finding the way.*
— iAjay J.

Introduction

Youth is a fire — bright, restless, searching.

This book is a journey across the inner world of today's generation. Every poem in these pages is a mirror. Sometimes it will show your struggle, sometimes your strength, sometimes your deepest truth.

May these words guide you, not as rules, but as reminders: that your journey is yours, your dreams are worthy, and your heart already holds the answers.

This book gives **collection of 24-poems**:

Phase 1: The Restless Beginning (youth struggles & search)

Phase 2: Love & Connection (relationships & emotions)

Phase 3: Growth & Maturity (inner strength & wisdom)

Phase 4: Responsibility & Purpose (clarity & legacy)

This full arc touches **every major emotion of today's youth.**

❖ Phase 1:

The Restless Beginning

(The Search for Identity and Direction)

It includes:

- 💭 **The Unfinished Dream** — the drifting thoughts that never let sleep settle.
- 🧠 **The Weight I Carry** — every burden invisible, but heavy still.
- ⬜ **Mirror, Mirror** — reflection blurred by what the world wants to see.
- 🏃 **Race Without Finish Line** — running endlessly, chasing a mirage of "enough."
- 🌪 **Noise in My Head** — a storm louder than any crowd outside.
- ⬜ **Still Finding the Way** — the compass spinning, yet pointing home within.

1. The Unfinished Dream (Dreams vs. Distractions)

I dream of skies too wide to hold,
of stories waiting to be told.
But every step, a screen pulls near,
a thousand voices drown the clear.

I plan to climb, I plan to start,
yet scrolling steals the lion's heart.
The hours vanish, thin as air,
dreams grow faint, yet still are there.

Distractions wear a painted face,
promising joy but stealing grace.
They whisper softly, "Stay awhile,"
while destiny waits another mile.

But dreams are seeds that beg for rain,
they wilt if fed with idle gain.
So I must choose with steady will,
the noise to drop, the climb to fill.

For when the curtain falls at last,
it won't be likes or memes that last.
Only the dream I dared to chase,
will carve my name in time's embrace.

2. The Weight I Carry (Expectations & Pressure)

They hand me crowns I did not choose,
their victories shine, my dreams must lose.
A future planned before my birth,
a life defined by someone's worth.

Each question asked becomes a chain,
"Be the best, don't bring us shame."
But how can I bloom in borrowed light,
when my own seeds are kept from sight?

I wear their hopes upon my back,
a heavy load, a tightening track.
Smiles outside, but deep inside,
a child just wanting to decide.

Yet maybe strength is learning this:
to walk my path, not what they wish.
To prove that love is not a grade,
but in the choices I have made.

So I will bow, but not obey,
I'll find my truth, I'll carve my way.
For dreams are not a debt to pay,
but wings I'll grow to fly someday.

⊠ 3. Mirror, Mirror
(Identity & Comparison)

They told me beauty wears one face,
a flawless skin, a perfect grace.
But mirrors twist and screens deceive,
they sell us lies we start to believe.

I chase a look that isn't mine,
a borrowed mask, a thin design.
Yet every soul, unique, profound,
is worth more gold than world-renowned.

Comparison steals, it leaves me blind,
to treasures in my own design.
So let the mirror speak anew,
"Be only you — that's enough, that's true."

🏁 4. Race Without Finish Line (Chasing Success)

They push, they pull, they set the pace,
a thousand runners in one race.
Degrees, careers, the endless climb,
a finish line that hides in time.

We sprint for gold, we grasp for more,
but every win unlocks a door.
Another task, another prize,
success keeps shifting in disguise.

So what is gain if peace is lost?
What's worth the crown at such a cost?
The truest race is not to win,
but to be whole in my own skin.

5. Noise in My Head (Mental Health & Overthinking)

The night is loud, though all is still,
my thoughts, they crowd, they bend my will.
Each "what if" sharp, each "maybe" deep,
they steal my breath, they steal my sleep.

I wear a smile, but none can see,
the storms that rage inside of me.
Yet healing starts the day I say,
"I'm not okay — and that's okay."

For silence grows when truth is near,
when open hearts replace the fear.
So let the noise be named, be known,
and slowly, I'll be whole, my own.

⊠ 6. Still Finding the Way (Self-Discovery)

They ask me where I want to go,
what life to lead, what seeds to sow.
But how can maps be drawn so soon,
when I'm still learning sun and moon?

I do not fail by not yet clear,
the path will show when time is near.
For life's not meant to be a race,
but step by step, a sacred pace.

So let me wander, let me roam,
for every road still leads me home.
The way is found, both lost and free,
in learning who I'm meant to be.

💖 Phase 2:
Love & Connection

~~~~~~~~

(Heart, Friendship, and Belonging)

It includes:

- ✉ **Swipe Left, Swipe Right** — hearts meeting through screens, fading through swipes.
- ⊠ **The Empty Chair** — a seat that waits, echoing the warmth once shared.
- 🦋 **Breaking, Yet Beautiful** — love shatters, but the soul blooms again.
- ▢ **Echo Chamber** — voices loud, yet meaning lost in mirrors of screens.
- 🌸 **Masks We Wear** — smiling faces hiding silent truths beneath.
- ⊠ **A Place to Belong** — where hearts find home beyond judgment.

✉ 7. Swipe Left, Swipe Right (Modern Love)

Profiles bright, but hearts are dim,
we chase the spark, yet lose within.
A swipe, a match, a fleeting flame,
but love is more than just a game.

For true connection takes its time,
not shallow words or borrowed lines.
Love waits beyond the fleeting night,
a steady glow, a lasting light.

We crave a soul that feels like home,
not texts that fade when left alone.
For love's not found in pixels' gleam,
but in the silence — where hearts dream.

⊠ 8. The Empty Chair (Loneliness vs. True Friendship)

~~~

The crowd was full, the noise was loud,
yet still I felt outside the crowd.
A thousand names, but none who stay,
a thousand texts that fade away.

But friendship isn't numbers shown,
it's one true soul that feels like home.
So better one who truly cares,
than crowded rooms with empty chairs.

I've learned that peace can softly grow,
in quiet hearts that take it slow.
Not every silence means you're lost,
some love is calm — and worth the cost.

For noise can drown what hearts should hear,
the gentle ones who hold you near.

They speak in ways the world forgets —
in listening eyes, in no regrets.

So if you find that steady friend,
whose warmth the storms of time can't bend —
hold them close, and you will see,
you've found the truest company.

9. Breaking, Yet Beautiful (Heartbreak & Healing)

A heart can crack, a heart can bleed,
but brokenness is not defeat.
For even glass, when torn apart,
reflects new light, a brighter start.

The pain will fade, the scars will show,
but from the cracks, new strength will grow.
For heartbreak is not just the end,
it is the place where souls begin.

The tears once burned, but now they cleanse,
they wash away what never mends.
From empty hands and shattered dreams,
rise wiser hearts with gentler schemes.

So let it break, let sorrow speak,
for even grief can make us seek.

What once was loss now softly proves,
we heal through pain — and learn to love.

And when at last the storm is through,
you'll find the sky a softer blue.
For every crack the heart endured,
let in the light — and left it cured.

📱 10. Echo Chamber (Social Media Illusions)

We post, we scroll, we play the part,
a filtered life, a crafted art.
But likes can't fill the aching void,
a truthless joy is soon destroyed.

Behind the screens, behind the show,
we long for love, for depth to grow.
So let me live, not just display,
a life that's real in night and day.

The world applauds the perfect frame,
yet hides the tears that look the same.
We trade our peace for fleeting fame,
forgetting hearts aren't built for games.

So here I stand, both raw and true,
with flaws that shine like morning dew.
No lens can hold what souls convey —
I'll live my truth, unframed, each day.

🎭 11. Masks We Wear (Authenticity vs. Pretending)

I smile, I laugh, I play along,
but underneath, it all feels wrong.
A mask I wear to fit the crowd,
yet silence screams beneath too loud.

But masks will crack, they always do,
and what is left must still be you.
So better raw, imperfect, real,
than polished lies you cannot feel.

The world rewards the painted face,
yet hides the truth we dare not face.
We chase approval, lose our spark,
and call it light while living dark.

To stand unmasked takes quiet grace,
to love yourself, your truest face.

For those who stay when veils are gone —
are the ones who've seen the real you all along.

So drop the mask, let softness show,
be who you are, let spirit glow.
For life begins where falsehood ends,
and truth itself becomes your friend.

⊠ 12. A Place to Belong (Community & Acceptance)

The world feels vast, the road too wide,
I search for hearts where I can hide.
A place that says, "You are enough,"
through gentle hands, through tender love.

And when I find that sacred space,
acceptance shines, a soft embrace.
For every soul deserves a song,
a place to stay, a place belong.

Not built of walls or fancy halls,
but hearts that answer when one calls.
Where silence speaks, and eyes reveal,
the kind of truth no words can seal.

For home's not found, it's softly made,
in kindness shared, in fears allayed.
In every heart that lights your way —
belonging blooms, and chooses to stay.

🔥 Phase 3: Growth & Maturity

(Strength, Resilience, and Wisdom)

It includes:

- 🌿 **Fall Forward** — falling not backward, but into lessons that lift.
- 🕯️ **Slow Flames** — steady burns that outlast every storm.
- 🌑 **The Leap** — faith unfolding its wings mid-air.
- 🍽️ **The Empty Feast** — when plenty fills the plate but not the heart.
- ⏳ **The Hourglass** — grains of gold slipping through unaware hands.
- 🌙 **Alone, Not Lonely** — silence becoming music within the soul.

🌿 13. Fall Forward (Power of Failure)

I stumbled hard, I hit the ground,
the world grew still, no hope around.
But in that fall, I came to see,
failure was not the end of me.

It carved my pride, it stripped my lies,
it taught me where true courage lies.
Each broken step became a tool,
each scar a lesson, sharp but cruel.

So let me fall, and fall once more,
each time I'll rise, each time I'll soar.
For failure's gift is clear, profound —
it builds the wings from broken ground.

14. Slow Flames (Patience in Progress)

We crave the lightning, fast and bright,
but growth is gentle, out of sight.
A seed does not become a tree,
without the hours of mystery.

The world may rush, but truth is slow,
the roots must spread before they show.
And every flame that burns for years,
is kindled small through sweat and tears.

So let me walk, not run, my way,
for slow flames warm more than they slay.
The patient climb, the steady breath,
creates a life that conquers death.

🦅 15. The Leap (Overcoming Fear)

Fear whispers loud, "Stay where you are,
the ground is safe, the sky too far."
But freedom waits beyond the edge,
across the cliffs, beyond the ledge.

I feel my knees begin to shake,
my hands are weak, my bones might break.
Yet still I jump, I still must try,
for wings are born when feet defy.

So let me leap, though shadows scream,
though doubt may haunt this fragile dream.
For fear may roar, but hope is higher —
and leaps alone ignite the fire.

🍽 16. The Empty Feast
(Greed vs. Contentment)

A table full, yet hearts are bare,
we gather wealth, but lose our care.
The gold we clutch can't feed the soul,
a hungry heart is never whole.

We chase for more, but more decays,
enough is lost in endless craze.
Contentment sings a softer tune,
a gentle sun, a lasting moon.

So let my joy be small, but true,
not what I own, but what I do.
For greed consumes, but peace will feast,
on humble bread, the greatest feast.

⌛ 17. The Hourglass (Time as Currency)

I spent my minutes like falling sand,
they slipped too fast through careless hands.
The hours fled, the days grew thin,
and never once returned again.

We waste on screens, on fleeting praise,
forgetting life is counted days.
No currency is worth this gold,
the ticking clock we cannot hold.

So let me spend each breath with care,
with love to give, with time to spare.
For time once lost will not repeat,
its footsteps fade, its march complete.

☽ 18. Alone, Not Lonely (The Beauty of Solitude)

The crowd grew loud, the world too near,
yet silence called, and I could hear.
Alone, I found a softer song,
a place where I could just belong.

No masks to wear, no stage to play,
just me, myself, at end of day.
And in that stillness, truth was born,
a gentle dawn, a quiet morn.

So solitude, my dearest friend,
you teach me how the soul can mend.
For loneliness is empty fear,
but being alone makes vision clear.

☆ Phase 4: Responsibility & Purpose

(Legacy, Purpose, and Peace)

It includes:

- 🤍 **Echoes of Kindness** – gentle acts that ripple farther than we see.
- 🔥 **Voice Unshaken** – truth steady, even when the world trembles.
- 🌳 **Roots and Wings** – grounded by love, yet free to soar.
- ⊠ **The Compass Within** – direction born not from maps, but meaning.
- 🕯 **Legacy of Light** – passing the flame, not the weight.
- 🕊 **The Journey Home** – realizing we've always been walking inward

19. Echoes of Kindness

(Compassion & Empathy)

A gentle word, a helping hand,
can heal a wound, can help one stand.
No act too small, no smile too weak,
a kindness plants the hope we seek.

For long after our voices fade,
the echoes of our love are made.
The world is built not on the strong,
but hearts that choose to right the wrong.

When tempers rise and harsh words burn,
be still enough to pause — to learn.
For grace begins where pride has died,
and peace is born when hearts collide.

One spark of care can light the skies,
it lives through tears, through last goodbyes.
For love outlives the fleeting years —
it blooms in souls, it softens fears.

🔥 20. Voice Unshaken (Courage to Speak Up)

The silence weighs, it feels so safe,
but truth untold becomes a grave.
The world won't change with whispered lies,
but with the fire in honest eyes.

So speak, though tremors shake your chest,
your voice may spark a soul's unrest.
For one small word, both fierce and true,
can break the chains for more than you.

For every truth the brave ones share,
a thousand hearts will breathe fresh air.
The world is waiting, scared, yet near —
for voices strong enough to hear.

Don't fear the cracks your truth may start,
they're just the openings of the heart.
For silence ends where courage sings,
and freedom grows on fearless wings.

21. Roots and Wings (Tradition & Change)

My roots run deep, they ground my soul,
they give me strength, they make me whole.
But wings must spread, must claim the sky,
for dreams can't live if roots deny.

I'll honor past, yet still create,
a future bold, a widened gate.
For life is both — to hold, to fly,
to keep the ground, yet kiss the sky.

⊠ 22. The Compass Within (Finding Purpose)

I chased the maps, I chased the signs,
I followed roads of others' lines.
But every path that wasn't mine,
just left me lost in borrowed time.

Then silence spoke, the heart replied,
"My compass waits, it lives inside."
And once I turned to what was true,
my purpose rose — a clearer view.

The world still whispers, "This is best,"
but now I trust my inner quest.
For purpose isn't found or planned,
it grows each time I understand.

No trophies shine like peace of mind,
no finish line, no race to find.
For those who walk their own pure way,
will never drift, though skies turn gray.

23. Legacy of Light (Responsibility for the Future)

What will remain when I am gone?
A fleeting name, a forgotten song?
Or seeds I sow in minds I've touched,
a brighter world, a kinder trust?

The future waits on what I give,
the way I choose, the way I live.
So let my legacy be light,
a torch to carry through the night.

Not monuments of stone or fame,
but hearts that whisper still my name.
For gentle acts, though small they seem,
can outlive gold, can shape a dream.

And when the dusk dissolves to dawn,
my flame will spark in those who've gone —

not as a shadow, dim or slight,
but as their own new wings of light.

For love once shared will never fade,
it lives in lives that others made.
So let my story softly stay —
a light that leads another's way.

24. The Journey Home (Peace & Acceptance)

At last I see, the path was kind,
each twist and turn shaped heart and mind.
The race was never to arrive,
but to be present, to feel alive.

No gold, no crown, no fleeting fame,
can weigh against love's gentle flame.
For home was never far or gone —
it lived inside my soul all along.

And now I walk with lighter feet,
no past to chase, no pain to beat.
For peace was not a place to find,
but a garden grown within my mind.

Closing Note

Life is not a sprint, nor a straight road. It is a spiral —
each lesson returns until it is learned.
If you've seen yourself in these poems, it means you're
alive, aware, and already growing.

The world does not need you to be perfect.
It needs you to be **real, kind, and brave enough to live
your truth**.